FEDERAL RESERVE SYSTEM

AGENTS OF  GOVERNMENT

VALERIE BODDEN

Creative Education • Creative Paperbacks

Published by Creative Education and Creative Paperbacks
P.O. Box 227, Mankato, Minnesota 56002
Creative Education and Creative Paperbacks are
imprints of The Creative Company
www.thecreativecompany.us

Design and production by Chelsey Luther
Art direction by Rita Marshall

Printed in Malaysia

Photographs by Alamy (epa european pressphoto agency b.v.), Corbis (Jean-Louis Atlan/
Sygma, Bettmann, Bob Daemmrich/Bob Daemmrich Photography, Inc., Jonathan Ernst/
Reuters, Ashley Gilbertson/VII, Lynn Goldsmith, John Greim/LOOP IMAGES, Vincent
Laforet/Pool/Reuters, TANNEN MAURY/epa, Minnesota Historical Society, Museum of the
City of New York, LM Otero/AP, H. Armstrong Roberts/ClassicStock, Axel Schmies/Novarc,
Michel Setboun, Adam Stoltman, Underwood & Underwood, Oscar White), deviantART
(AllydNYC), Dreamstime (fstockfoto, Steveheap), Getty Images (Bloomberg, Ed Freeman,
Keystone-France, Thomas D. McAvoy), Shutterstock (American Spirit, AngeloNZ,
Kjpargeter)

Library of Congress Cataloging-in-Publication Data
Bodden, Valerie.
Federal Reserve system / Valerie Bodden.
p. cm. — (Agents of government)
Summary: An in-depth look at the people and policies behind the government agency known
as the Fed, from its founding in 1913 to the controversies and challenges it faces today.
Includes bibliographical references and index.

ISBN 978-1-60818-546-7 (hardcover)
ISBN 978-1-62832-147-0 (pbk)
1. Federal Reserve banks. I. Title.

HG2563.B5746 2015
332.1'10973—dc23   2014029606

CCSS: RI.5.1, 2, 3, 5, 6, 8; RH.6-8.3, 4, 5, 8

First Edition HC 9 8 7 6 5 4 3 2 1
First Edition PBK 9 8 7 6 5 4 3 2 1

TABLE OF CONTENTS

On December 23, 1913, president Woodrow Wilson picked up a gold pen and signed into law the Federal Reserve Act.

It had taken members of Congress more than five years—and a lot of debate—to develop the act. The new law established the Federal Reserve as a central bank for the United States. As he signed the bill, President Wilson said he was grateful to have a part in creating the new organization. He believed it would be "of lasting benefit to the business of the country." The Federal Reserve was established in response to banking panics that rocked the American **economy** in the late 1800s and early 1900s. The purpose of the Federal Reserve was to prevent such panics by controlling the country's money supply. In the more than 100 years of its existence, the role of the Federal Reserve (also known as the Fed) has expanded significantly. It now plays a major part in the U.S. economy. Unlike most other government agencies, the Fed operates independently. The Fed's independence—as well as its response to various financial crises—has earned it both praise and criticism over the years. Today, the role of the country's central bank remains as controversial as at its founding.

Another act President Wilson signed into law in 1913 provided for America's first federal income tax.

Getting Started

The Federal Reserve was not the nation's first attempt at a central bank—a government bank to control the nation's money supply. Two previous central banks had been established, one in 1791 and the other in 1816. Each had lasted for 20 years before closing. The first bank was troubled by fraud. The second was closed by president Andrew Jackson.

For a time, America went without a central bank. Hundreds of banks across the country issued their own colorful **banknotes**, and **counterfeit** money was everywhere. Banks were only loosely regulated. Many made risky loans. Some did not keep enough money in their reserve accounts   the accounts used to clear customers' checks or provide customers with **currency**.

These conditions led to banking panics in the late 1800s and early 1900s. Panics were often sparked by rumors that a bank owner had gotten into financial trouble in the **stock market**. Nervous customers would make a run on the bank. That is, they would pull their money out of the bank. In many cases, the bank did not have enough money to pay all its customers. As a re-

During the Panic of 1893, "bank runs" became common as hundreds of banks closed throughout the country.

sult, the bank failed, or went out of business. As word of one bank's failure spread, people made runs on other banks. They knew that if they did not get their deposits out before the bank failed, they would never see that money again.

The most severe banking panic occurred in 1907. It spurred a new attempt at the creation of a central bank. In May 1908, Congress established the National Monetary Commission to study the U.S. banking system. It was headed by senator Nelson Aldrich. In November 1910, Aldrich held a secret meeting with a number of bankers to make a plan for a central bank. The meeting was kept quiet because Aldrich feared that Americans would not like a plan that had been crafted by bankers. He was right. Many Americans opposed the plan, which called for a central bank led by a board of bankers. Most believed this would give financial institutions too much power. Congress made a number of changes to the plan. In place of a single central bank, Congress called for several reserve banks to be set up across the country. Bankers opposed these changes. But this version of the plan became the basis for the Federal Reserve Act, which was passed in 1913.

Federal Reserve banks were established in 12 cities: Boston, New York, Philadelphia, Cleveland, Richmond, Atlanta, Chicago, St. Louis, Minneapolis, Kansas City, Dallas, and San Francisco. The banks opened on November 16, 1914, less than a year after the Federal Reserve Act had been signed. "The opening of these banks marks a new era in the history of business and finance in this country," U.S. Treasury secretary William McAdoo said. "It is believed that they will put an end to the annual anxiety from which the country has suffered for the past generation."

The main purpose of the newly established Fed was to create an "elastic" currency. This meant that the Fed would control the amount of money in the economy according to the country's needs. In addition, reserve banks would hold the reserves of their local member banks, making the money easy for banks to access. And if a bank ran short on reserves, the reserve bank would serve as "lender of last resort" and provide a loan to the bank. The Federal Reserve also established a new, standardized banknote. It set up a national check-clearing system and regulated member banks.

Not all banks were members of the Federal

> *"The opening of these banks marks a new era in the history of business and finance in this country."*

Bank security was serious business in the early 1900s, reflecting anxieties about the industry and robberies.

MULLERS
EMPLOYMENT
AGENCY
1 FLIGHT UP
OTTO BECK, Lic.

*Employment agencies in
big cities were daily
overrun with people
looking for work—of any
kind—during the 1930s.*

Reserve, though. Banks with national **charters** were required to join the Fed. But banks with state charters did not have to become part of the Federal Reserve System. Only about one-third of all **commercial** banks in the country joined the new system. Membership in the Federal Reserve gave banks the right to borrow funds from the Fed and to receive check-processing and money-delivery services. In return, member banks were required to purchase **stock** in their local reserve bank. They also had to keep a minimum level of reserves in the reserve bank and follow stricter banking regulations.

The Fed opened for business just after the start of World War I. In 1917 and 1918, when the U.S. became involved in the war, it helped sell **bonds** to the public. Money raised by the bonds paid for wartime expenses. Later, when Americans wanted to redeem their bonds, the government would pay back the cost of the bond plus **interest**. Thus, the government wanted interest rates to remain low. Although the Fed was an independent agency within the government, it followed the government's request.

After the war, the Fed raised interest rates, leading to a brief **recession**. The U.S. economy soon recovered, however, and boomed throughout the 1920s. Most agreed that, so far, the Fed had been a success. It had helped the U.S. economy grow, prevented financial crises, and established the dollar as one of the world's top currencies.

The booming economy led many Americans to take out loans to buy houses and make other large purchases. Many also borrowed money to invest in the stock market. At first, the stock market took off. But members of the Fed were nervous that the market high couldn't last. In 1928 and 1929, they raised interest rates in an attempt to slow borrowing. The rising interest rates caused stock prices to fluctuate. People got anxious and began to sell off their stocks. In October 1929, the stock market crashed. America had entered the Great Depression.

In recent years, the Fed has taken responsibility for contributing to the Great Depression. "Regarding the Great Depression,... we did it. We're very sorry.... We won't do it again," said

"Regarding the Great Depression,...
we did it. We're very sorry....
We won't do it again."

Ben Bernanke, who served as chairman of the Fed from 2006 to 2014.

The economic decline led to a series of banking panics, beginning in November 1930. Many Americans lost their life savings, their jobs, and their homes. Meanwhile, members of the Federal Reserve Board of Governors argued about how to respond to the crisis. Some Board members believed the Fed should fulfill its role as lender of last resort and provide needed loans to troubled banks. But others thought weak banks should be allowed to fail in order to strengthen the overall banking system. Still others believed that the way to end the Depression was to keep money out of the economy by preventing loans to banks. With so much disagreement, the Fed failed to take decisive action to help banks in need.

The Great Depression led to a number of reforms in America's banking industry and in the Federal Reserve. The Banking Acts of 1933 and 1935 separated commercial banks and investment firms. They also created the Federal Deposit Insurance Corporation (FDIC) to insure customers' bank deposits. The acts gave the Board of Governors, located in Washington, D.C., some of the power that had rested with the district reserve banks. The 1935 act also changed the leadership structure of the Board. The secre-

AGENCY INSIDER

PAUL VOLCKER

Paul Volcker served as president of the New York Federal Reserve from 1975 to 1979. In August 1979, he was appointed chairman of the Board of Governors. During his chairmanship, Volcker helped to bring down record-high **inflation** levels. After leaving the Board in 1987, Volcker became part-owner of a financial services firm. From 2009 to 2011, he chaired President Obama's Economic Recovery Advisory Board. He helped to shape the Dodd–Frank Act to reform the Fed and the financial system.

Treasury secretary and Fed chairman Andrew Mellon (far left) resisted using federal funds to relieve the depressed economy.

Successful sales of World War I bonds (shown) prompted the government to pursue a similar plan in the 1940s.

tary of the U.S. Treasury and the comptroller of the currency had previously served as members of the Board. But they were now replaced by a chairman and vice chairman appointed by the U.S. president.

When World War II began in 1939, it stimulated the U.S. economy. As in World War I, the Fed helped with the war effort by keeping interest rates on war bonds low. But when the war ended, the Fed wanted to raise interest rates to fight inflation. President Harry Truman and the Treasury Department wanted the rates to remain low. In 1951, the Fed and the Treasury came to an agreement known as the Treasury–Federal Reserve Accord. The accord freed the Fed from keeping interest rates low and allowed it to act independently. In doing so, it helped establish the Fed's leading role in modern monetary policy.

FEDERAL RESERVE
Washington, D.C., U.S.A.

The operations of the Federal Reserve in Washington, D.C., are housed in two buildings named for former Fed chairpersons. The Marriner S. Eccles Building was completed in 1937 and named after Eccles in 1982. Meetings of the Board of Governors are held in its large boardroom. The William McChesney Martin Jr. Building is located across the street. This building was completed in 1974 to provide more space for the Fed's growing responsibilities. The two buildings are linked by an underground tunnel.

OUR JOBS FLEW AWAY, LETS SEND Reagan FLYING
GIVE PEOPLE DIGNITY GIVE THEM JOBS
STAY THE COURSE LOSE EVERYTHING!
SENATOR!!!
Union Jobs
union wages
UNEMPLOYED COMMITTEE

Too High, Too Low, and Just Right

Throughout most of the 1950s and '60s, the American economy remained stable. But in the late 1960s, the Fed allowed the amount of money in the economy to grow, resulting in a steep rise in inflation. At the same time, unemployment levels began to go up. Inflation and unemployment remained high from the late 1960s through the early 1980s. This period became known as the Great Inflation.

By 1980, unemployment had reached 7.5 percent, and inflation was at 14.5 percent. The Humphrey–Hawkins Act of 1978 had tasked the Fed with keeping both unemployment and inflation levels at 3 percent or less. But the Fed could not figure out how to bring one level down without increasing the other. When it lowered interest rates, businesses were able to take out loans to expand and create jobs. But at the same time, inflation increased. In response, the Fed would raise interest rates to fight inflation. This prompted businesses to cut jobs. According to finance professor Jeremy Siegel, the Great Inflation marked "the greatest failure of American macroeconomic policy" since the Great Depression.

Unemployment woes in the 1980s spurred demonstrations in the nation's capital akin to those in the Depression era.

In August 1979, Paul Volcker was appointed chairman of the Federal Reserve Board of Governors. Volcker had previously served as head of the Federal Reserve Bank of New York. He believed that bringing down inflation should be the Fed's number-one priority. It was only by controlling inflation, he said, that the unemployment rate would eventually be brought down.

On October 6, 1979, Volcker announced a new approach to monetary policy. Instead of focusing on interest rates, the Fed would decrease the amount of money in the economy by requiring banks to keep a high level of reserves. Volcker knew this might lead to a recession. In fact, he hoped it would and "the sooner the better," so inflation would come down. Volcker also predicted that unemployment would rise temporarily as a result. He was right. The economy entered a recession, and the unemployment rate rose to a postwar record-high 10 percent.

People across the country expressed their hatred for Volcker. Farmers protested outside the Federal Reserve's headquarters, and Volcker was given Secret Service protection. Republican George Hansen, representative from Idaho, even accused the Fed of "destroying the American dream."

But Volcker held his course. "Failure to carry through now in the fight on inflation will only make any subsequent effort more difficult," he said. Volcker's strategy worked. By 1983, inflation levels had decreased to 3 percent. Unemployment levels soon began to fall as well.

Volcker's tenure as Fed chairman also saw the passage of one of the most important bills in the Fed's history. The Depository Institutions Deregulation and Monetary Control Act of 1980 gave the Fed greater power over the nation's money supply. It required even nonmember banks, credit unions, and other institutions to hold a certain level of reserves at their district reserve bank. It also allowed nonmember banks to borrow from the Fed.

From the mid-1980s to 2007, the U.S. economy experienced a period of stability. Inflation and unemployment remained low as the economy boomed. Economists came to call this period the Great Moderation. Many credited the Fed with helping to create the conditions that made such economic stability possible. When financial crises threatened, the Fed was quick to respond. In October 1987, the

Economists came to call this period the Great Moderation.

The Fed's response to a 1987 stock market crash led banks calmly out of a downward spiral and renewed confidence.

PANIC!

plunges through floor — 508 pt

PAGES OF COMPLETE COVERAGE BEGIN ON PAGE 2

ANTHONY PESCAT*

GETS 6 MONTHS

charge   Story on page

As stores and other businesses closed during the Great Recession, properties sat empty, waiting for better times.

stock market crashed. New Fed chairman Alan Greenspan assured the country that the Fed was ready to provide **credit** to banks as needed.

In 1999, the Fed's powers were again expanded with the passage of the Gramm–Leach–Bliley Act. This act removed the earlier separation between banks and investment firms. It allowed for the creation of financial holding companies, which could offer banking, insurance, and investment services. The Fed was to serve as the regulator for these new institutions. However, in the years to come, many people would question whether the Fed had done its job. According to economist Richard A. Posner, during this time, the Fed was "asleep at the switch." Posner and others believe that the Fed's lack of oversight led to a financial crisis that began in 2007. This crisis came to be known as the Great Recession.

The Great Recession had its roots in low interest rates, which the Fed instituted in 2001 to fight a brief recession. Even after the economy recovered, though, the Fed kept interest rates low. Low interest rates meant that banks could offer more loans. Many banks began to offer subprime loans. These were loans to people with poor financial histories, little money for a down payment on a mortgage, or high levels of debt.

As banks handed out more loans, the demand for houses increased, fueling a rise in home prices. But in 2007, a major subprime mortgage company filed for **bankruptcy**. Many others followed. As a result, a large number of banks stopped making subprime loans. With fewer loans being made, the demand for houses fell. So did home prices. Many people tried to sell homes they could no longer afford. But often the homes were worth 20 to 30 percent less than their owners had paid for them. Thousands of homes went into **foreclosure** as more people became unable to make mortgage payments.

The collapse of the housing market led to a recession that lasted until 2009. During this time, the unemployment rate reached 10 percent. Ben Bernanke, who had taken over as Fed chairman in 2006, knew the Fed had to act. "I knew that if the global financial system were to collapse, ... we would be facing, potentially,

...in the years to come, many people would question whether the Fed had done its job.

another depression of the severity and length of the Depression in the 1930s," he later explained.

So the Fed took drastic action to keep the country's biggest financial firms from failing. It lowered the interest rate to near zero. It handed out emergency loans to financial institutions. It helped the financial company JPMorgan Chase take over the failing investment bank Bear Stearns. It also provided credit to keep the large insurance company AIG in business. The Fed took these actions, known as bailouts, because it believed these financial companies were "too big to fail." In other words, if these businesses failed, they would take down a number of small-er businesses connected to them. Many credit the Fed's actions with preventing an economic collapse. At the same time, there was an outcry among those who did not believe the govern-ment should use public funds to support private companies. President Barack Obama pointed out that bailouts "left taxpayers on the hook if a big bank or financial institution ever failed."

In order to prevent another major crisis—and further bailouts—in 2010, Congress passed the Dodd–Frank Act, the country's biggest financial overhaul since the post-Depression regulations. Among other things, the act brought large nonbank financial organizations under the Fed's

AGENCY INSIDER

MARRINER ECCLES

After earning a law degree, Marriner Eccles en-tered the banking world. During the heart of the Great Depression, he gained fame for keeping his bank from failing. He was appointed chairman of the Federal Reserve Board of Governors in 1934. In this role, he helped to draft the Banking Act of 1935, which changed the structure of the Fed. After resigning the chairmanship in 1948, Eccles remained on the Board until 1951. He then returned to commercial banking. He died in 1977.

In a movement called *Occupy Wall Street* that began in 2011, protesters called for banking and other reforms.

oversight. It also attempted to get rid of the too-big-to-fail concept and created the new Consumer Financial Protection Bureau.

Although the Federal Reserve implements laws such as Dodd–Frank, the Fed is considered "independent within the government." This means that while the Fed is part of the government, it does not take orders from Congress or the president in setting monetary policy. Even so, the Fed is subject to Congressional oversight, and its actions must be in agreement with the overall financial policies set by Congress.

Members of the public may not deal directly with the Federal Reserve, but its actions affect people across the U.S.—and the world. The interest rate the Fed charges banks has an impact on the interest rates banks charge their customers. Interest rate changes also affect whether companies expand and hire more workers or let people go. These decisions guide economic growth and individuals' decisions about spending and saving. Changes in the interest rate also influence the price of U.S. goods sold in other countries and the price of foreign products sold in the U.S.

Beginning his presidency amidst the Great Recession, Barack Obama looked for ways to protect businesses and the public.

FEDERAL RESERVE BANK of
New York, U.S.A.

The Federal Reserve Bank of New York is headquartered in a 22-story building that fills nearly an entire city block. Completed in 1924, the New York Fed today houses what is believed to be the world's largest concentration of gold. The gold belongs to foreign countries, foreign central banks, and other international institutions. The gold vault lies 80 feet (24.4 m) below the streets of New York City and is surrounded by thick walls of steel and concrete. It is open to the public for tours.

Boards, Committees, and Banks, Oh My

The Fed is a central bank. That means it is a bank that serves banks rather than the public. The Fed has four main areas of responsibility: conducting monetary policy; supervising and regulating banks and protecting consumers; maintaining a stable financial system; and providing financial services to banks and the U.S. government.

In order to carry out those duties, the Fed employs more than 20,000 people. The Federal Reserve System consists of the Board of Governors in Washington, D.C., the Federal Open Market Committee (FOMC), and 12 district Federal Reserve banks and their branches. As at the Fed's creation, all nationally chartered banks are required to become members of the Fed. State banks can choose to join as well. Altogether, the system provides services to more than 3,000 member banks—about one-third of all commercial banks in the country. It also regulates and provides services to about 17,000 nonmember banks, credit unions, and other financial institutions.

The Federal Reserve Board of Governors con-

The Federal Reserve Bank of New York has been housed in its fortress-like edifice constructed of stone since 1924.

sists of seven members. The members, known as governors, are appointed by the U.S. president and confirmed by the Senate. Each governor serves a 14-year, nonrenewable term. In January of every even-numbered year, one governor's term expires. While some governors are economists, others have a background in business, law, academia, manufacturing, or banking.

The Board of Governors is headed by a chairman and vice chairman. Both are appointed by the president and confirmed by the Senate. The chairman and vice chairman have to be current members of the Board. Or they must be appointed to the Board at the same time they are appointed to their positions. Both offices have a four-year term and can be reappointed.

The Board of Governors generally meets every other week. Unless the Board

While some governors are economists, others have a background in business, law, academia, manufacturing, or banking.

is discussing confidential, or private, financial matters, its meetings are open to the public. At the meetings, governors discuss and vote on Fed policies. Fed governors are responsible for monitoring and analyzing the state of the economy. They also supervise district Federal Reserve banks, regulate the U.S. banking system, and set reserve requirements for banks. In addition, they oversee consumer protection regulations.

The Board of Governors is supported by a staff of nearly 2,000 in Washington, D.C. This staff consists of economists, accountants, lawyers, and information technology experts. The Fed generally pays lower wages than private-sector, or nongovernment, jobs.

While the Board of Governors oversees most aspects of the Federal Reserve System, the FOMC sets the Fed's monetary policy. Its main role is to set a target for the federal funds rate. This is the rate banks pay to borrow reserve funds from other banks overnight (usually to cover checks that have been written that day). The FOMC consists of 12 members. All seven members of the Board of Governors sit on the FOMC, as does the president of the Federal Reserve Bank of New York. The presidents of the other Federal Reserve banks take turns serving on the FOMC. Four of them serve at a time. The chairman of the Board of Governors also serves as chairman of the FOMC. The president of the New York Fed acts as vice chairman. The FOMC is supported by more than 1,000 members from the Board of Governors' and district reserve banks' staffs.

Gary Gensler

Ben Bernanke
Chairman
Board of Governors of the
Federal Reserve System

In compliance with the Government in the Sunshine Act, the Board gives a one-week notice before open meetings.

Decisions from FOMC meetings can be broadcast directly to the trading floors, where responses are most immediate.

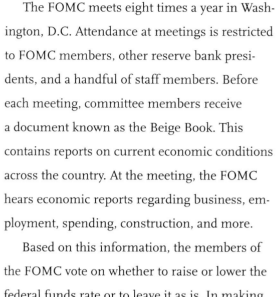

The FOMC meets eight times a year in Washington, D.C. Attendance at meetings is restricted to FOMC members, other reserve bank presidents, and a handful of staff members. Before each meeting, committee members receive a document known as the Beige Book. This contains reports on current economic conditions across the country. At the meeting, the FOMC hears economic reports regarding business, employment, spending, construction, and more.

Based on this information, the members of the FOMC vote on whether to raise or lower the federal funds rate or to leave it as is. In making such decisions, the FOMC must keep in mind the Fed's "dual **mandate**" to promote maximum employment and stable prices. In general, if the economy is moving slowly, the FOMC will vote to lower the federal funds rate. If inflation has become a problem, it might choose to raise it. The FOMC's actions will usually have an impact on the economy within 6 to 18 months. As the federal funds rate goes up, banks will charge their customers more interest. As it goes down, banks charge less interest.

In addition to the FOMC and Board of Governors, the Federal Reserve is made up of 12 Federal Reserve banks across the country. Each bank is responsible for serving and overseeing the banks in a particular district, based on borders drawn up by the Fed. A nine-member board of directors leads each Federal Reserve bank. Six of the board members are elected by member banks in the district. The other three, including the chairman, are appointed by the Board of Governors. Members of the board of directors come from a wide range of industries. Some are bankers. But others come from agriculture, business, or manufacturing. They serve on the board of their local reserve bank on a part-time basis. Every two weeks, they meet to set the discount rate. This is the interest rate at which banks can borrow funds from the reserve bank. The rate must be approved by the Board of Governors.

District board members also supervise the operations of the reserve bank. They select the bank president, who is also subject to approval by the Board in Washington, D.C. Reserve bank presidents are appointed to five-year, renewable

The FOMC's actions will usually have an impact on the economy within 6 to 18 months.

terms. They are the best-paid employees in the Fed, earning up to $410,000 a year. (The Board of Governors chairman earns around $200,000.) Most reserve banks have branches in other cities. These are overseen by their own boards.

The 12 Federal Reserve banks hold the reserves of the banks in their district. They also provide loans to member banks when needed. Millions of bills and coins pass through a reserve bank each year. The bank pulls damaged or worn money from circulation and issues new currency and coins from the U.S. Mint (coins) and the Bureau of Engraving and Printing (cur-

rency). Reserve banks also process checks and **wire transfers** and provide checking accounts for the U.S. Treasury. They send out inspectors to examine state-chartered member banks. (Other governmental organizations oversee non-member banks and federally chartered banks.) Staff economists at each reserve bank study local conditions and report them in the Beige Book. Reserve banks employ anywhere from 850 to 3,000 people.

Although each of the reserve banks plays a major role in the Federal Reserve System, the New York Fed is often considered the most important. It is responsible for carrying out the

AGENCY INSIDER

ALAN GREENSPAN

Alan Greenspan was appointed chairman of the Board of Governors in 1987. He served 5 terms before leaving the Board in January 2006 at the age of 79. Before joining the Federal Reserve, Greenspan served as an economic adviser to presidents Gerald Ford and Ronald Reagan. As Board chairman, Greenspan was praised for establishing a long period of economic growth. But he was blamed for failing to prevent events that led to the Great Recession. After leaving the Fed, Greenspan opened a consulting firm.

Federal printing facilities for U.S. currency are located in Fort Worth, Texas, and Washington, D.C.

decisions of the FOMC to raise or lower the federal funds rate. In order to do this, the New York Fed buys and sells government **securities**. This raises or lowers the amount of reserves in the system, which in turn affects interest rates. If the New York Fed buys securities, the reserve amount increases, and the federal funds rate goes down. If it sells securities, the reserve amount decreases, and the federal funds rate goes up. The New York Fed is also involved in foreign-exchange operations of buying and selling international currencies. In addition, many foreign governments store their gold reserves in vaults at the New York Fed.

Every year, the Federal Reserve System makes billions of dollars. Most of the money comes from interest on the government securities it buys and sells to adjust the federal funds rate. Other income is from loan interest paid by banks and service fees charged to banks and the Treasury. The Fed keeps just enough money to cover its operating expenses. It hands over the rest—almost $90 billion in 2012—to the U.S. Treasury.

The U.S. Treasury Building features a statue of fourth Treasury secretary Albert Gallatin on the north-side entrance.

RARIG'S KID
DOESN'T STARVE
WHY SHOULD WE?
AT TOO
WHY CA
GIVE MY
A JO

Keep It, Reform It, or Leave It?

At different times, the Fed has been either one of the most loved or one of the most hated U.S. government agencies. In many cases, the Fed has been blamed for significant financial crises, including the Great Depression, the Great Inflation, and the recent Great Recession. Still, many have pointed out that, even if the Fed has made mistakes, it has helped the country recover from financial crises. They say that without it, the nation might have been much worse off. According to former Fed staffer Jim Kudlinski, if the Fed were out of service "for even one day, the impact ... would be felt throughout this nation's and the world's economies." And if the Fed were gone forever, "it would be catastrophic."

Not everyone agrees. A 2009 survey showed that Americans believed the Fed had done the worst job of any government agency. Today, some people are calling for a major reform of the organization. Others want to get rid of it altogether.

To many economists, the biggest problem with the Fed is that its decisions are based on the judgments of the FOMC. They say that these rulings are not always consistent. Some econo-

The Great Depression deeply affected American families, and political groups seized any opportunity for demonstration.

mists have called on the Fed to develop rules to follow in setting monetary policy. During much of the Great Moderation, for example, the Fed acted in accordance with the Taylor Rule. This rule lays out a formula for determining what the interest rate should be based on current levels of inflation and unemployment. Those who favor a rule-based approach say that it would keep the Fed from holding interest rates too low or too high for too long.

Others say that the Fed's dual mandate is flawed. They believe the Fed should be tasked only with keeping prices and interest rates relatively stable. They do not think it should be expected to achieve employment goals for the country.

Still others propose reforming the Fed's lender-of-last-resort policy. Economist Allan Meltzer points out that the Fed has never clearly defined what it will or will not do as a lender of last resort. This may encourage some banks to participate in risky practices, expecting to receive a bailout if they fail. A clear policy would end such expectations. In addition, many believe that the Fed needs to be more careful about letting big banks combine to form megabanks that could be classified as too big to fail.

... the Fed has never clearly defined what it will or will not do as a lender of last resort.

Many opponents of the Fed object to its seemingly unlimited power. Some want to remove the Fed from its supervisory role over banks. They favor giving that job to another agency. Others want to limit the Fed's ability to make loans to banks. Some think the presidents of the reserve banks should be appointed by the U.S. president. Others want to make the Fed more accountable for its actions. Currently, the president has no right to remove a member of the Board of Governors from his or her position. But Meltzer proposes requiring the Board to announce a target for unemployment and inflation. Then, if it fails to meet that target within two or three years, the governors should have to explain why. They should also be willing to resign. Meltzer points out that in New Zealand and other countries that have instituted such policies, their central banks have placed more emphasis on meeting longer-term goals.

Even many of those who agree with the existence of the Federal Reserve oppose the policies it has adopted in the wake of the Great Recession. These policies include purchasing trillions of dollars' worth of securities and keeping the interest rate near zero for several

Originally built for CenTrust Savings Bank, the 47-story Miami Tower is somewhat typical of headquarters for modern banks.

Ron Paul's economic theories stem from his belief in an individual's freedom to choose—without government influence.

years. In 2012, the Fed announced that it would continue to hold the interest rate at that level at least through the middle of 2015. Opponents of this plan say that low interest rates slow down the economy and hurt small businesses and consumers whose savings earn little interest. They warn that pursuing the short-term goal of low interest rates has caused the Fed to overlook long-term dangers, such as inflation. Economist John Taylor, author of the Taylor Rule, is among those who disagree with Fed policies in response to the Great Recession. "[They are] experimental, and as I look at them, I'd see them as actually, basically negative," he said. Others contend that the Fed's policies have kept many Americans from losing their jobs.

While some people think that the Fed can be improved through policy changes, others want to do away with the system entirely. They argue that the Fed unintentionally weakens rather than helps the U.S. economy. The idea of a banking system without a central bank is referred to as free banking.

Former U.S. representative Ron Paul is one of the supporters of free banking. Paul says that in a free-banking system, banks would be forced to take responsibility for their own actions. Unsound banks would fail instead of being bailed out, and the overall banking system would be stronger as a result. Interest rates would be allowed to move freely. Without a central bank to interfere, supporters say, interest rates would naturally correct themselves. Low interest rates would lead to a higher demand for loans. A higher demand for loans, in turn, would bring interest rates up. When interest rates got too high, demand for loans would decrease. Then interest rates would fall again. Paul and many others who support free banking believe that the value of money should be based on the price of gold (as it was until the 1970s) or some other standard, such as the currency of a foreign country. Others argue that the size of the American economy would make such a system impossible.

The Federal Reserve is well aware of the criticisms leveled at it. In recent years, it has imple-

... in a free-banking system, banks would be forced to take responsibility for their own actions.

mented a number of reforms. In addition to supervising individual banks, the Fed has taken on the role of assessing the entire financial system. It looks for problems in large financial institutions that might put other organizations at risk. In order to do this, it has created the Office of Financial Stability Policy and Research as well as the Large Institution Supervision Coordinating Committee. The Fed has also added more than 150 employees to its banking supervision and regulation division. As part of its new regulations, the Fed now requires banks to draft plans for how they would respond if they began to fail.

Despite these changes, there are some things the Fed may never be able to fix. Forecasting economic activity is not an exact science. There is no way for the Fed to obtain up-to-the-minute economic information, so any information it acts on is incomplete. In addition, the markets' responses are often unpredictable. And the results of the Fed's actions are always delayed, making it difficult to determine the best time to act. On top of that, the Fed's decisions are not the only forces at play in the economy. Tax levels, natural disasters, the supply of goods, and other factors also have an influence.

AGENCY INSIDER

BEN BERNANKE

Ben Bernanke served as a professor of economics before joining the Board of Governors in 2002. He was appointed chairman in 2006 and is credited by many with leading the country through the Great Recession. But some economists criticized his policy of keeping interest rates low. Bernanke's second term as chairman ended in January 2014, and he was succeeded by Janet Yellen. After leaving the Fed, Bernanke worked for the Brookings Institution, a nonprofit policy research organization.

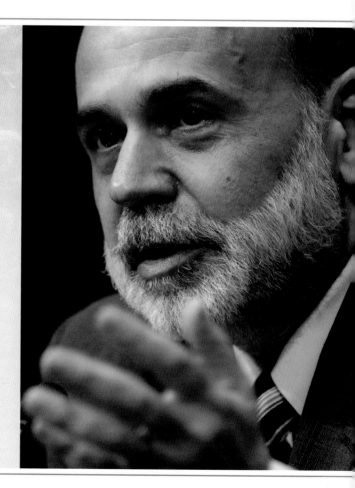

The physical devastation caused by Hurricane Katrina in 2005 also hampered economic recovery in New Orleans.

In the more than 100 years since it was founded, the Fed has grown in power and responsibility. It has had notable failures, including the Great Depression, the Great Inflation, and the Great Recession. But it has also had periods of success, such as the Great Moderation. Economists within the Fed continue to develop new methods to assess the U.S. economy and determine the best course for monetary policy. Whether the Fed remains as it is, undergoes reform, or is eventually ended remains to be seen. But one thing is certain: few governmental agencies have as important a role in managing our money as the Federal Reserve.

A general Federal Reserve System seal is featured on all U.S. currency today except the $1 and $2 bills.

FEDERAL RESERVE BANK of
SAN FRANCISCO, U.S.A.

The Federal Reserve Bank of San Francisco serves the largest geographical region of any Federal Reserve bank. It oversees banks in nine states (Alaska, Arizona, California, Hawaii, Idaho, Nevada, Oregon, Utah, and Washington), as well as U.S. island territories in the Pacific. It has branches in Los Angeles, Portland, Salt Lake City, and Seattle. In February 2014, former San Francisco Fed president Janet Yellen was appointed chairman of the Board of Governors. She was the first woman to hold that position.

GLOSSARY

banknotes paper money

bankruptcy a situation in which a business (or person) does not have enough money to pay all its debts; when a business files for bankruptcy, it is declared legally unable to pay its debts and is either closed down or reorganized

bonds documents through which the government or a company promises to pay back money it has borrowed, with interest

charters documents issued by the government authorizing a corporation or other organization to be established

commercial having to do with business; commercial banks take deposits from and make loans to businesses and individuals

counterfeit a realistic-looking copy of something, such as money, made for the purpose of deceiving

credit money provided by a bank and paid back at a future date

currency the system of money a country uses; currency often refers specifically to paper money

economy the system through which goods are produced, distributed, and consumed

foreclosure a legal process in which a bank takes back a home for which the homeowner is unable to make mortgage payments; the bank then tries to sell the home

inflation an overall increase in price levels across a wide range of products and services

interest an amount charged to borrow money; usually the interest charge is a percentage of the amount borrowed

macroeconomic having to do with large-scale economic conditions such as those of an entire country or region

mandate an instruction or command to do something

recession a period during which economic growth slows; recessions are often marked by high unemployment

securities certificates that show ownership of stocks or bonds

stock shared ownership in a company by many people who buy shares, or portions, of stock, hoping the company will make a profit and the stock value will increase

stock market a system for buying and selling stocks

wire transfers electronic movements of funds from one account to another

SELECTED BIBLIOGRAPHY

Axilrod, Stephen H. *Inside the Fed: Monetary Policy and Its Management, Martin through Greenspan to Bernanke.* Cambridge, Mass.: MIT Press, 2009.

Blinder, Alan S. *After the Music Stopped: The Financial Crisis, The Response, and the Work Ahead.* New York: Penguin, 2013.

Board of Governors of the Federal Reserve System. *The Federal Reserve System: Purposes and Function.* Washington, D.C.: Federal Reserve System, 2005.

Federal Reserve System. "Federal Reserve System: 100 Years." Federal Reserve System. 2013. http://www.federalreservehistory.org/.

Kudlinski, Jim. *The Tarnished Fed: Behind Closed Doors; Forty Years of Successes, Failures, Mystique, and Humor.* New York: Vantage, 2010.

Martin, Preston, and Lita Epstein. *The Complete Idiot's Guide to the Federal Reserve.* Indianapolis: Alpha, 2003.

Wells, Donald R. *The Federal Reserve System: A History.* Jefferson, N.C.: McFarland, 2004.

WEBSITES

Fed Chairman Game
http://sffed-education.org/chairman/
Try your hand at setting the federal funds rate. Watch how the changes you make affect the economy.

Federal Reserve Bank of Boston: Games and Online Learning
https://www.bostonfed.org/education/online/
Learn more about the economy with games, apps, and quizzes.

Note: Every effort has been made to ensure that the websites listed above are suitable for children, that they have educational value, and that they contain no inappropriate material. However, because of the nature of the Internet, it is impossible to guarantee that these sites will remain active indefinitely or that their contents will not be altered.

INDEX